Autism Spectrum Disorders

I. Victoria Susan

ATLANTIC

PUBLISHERS & DISTRIBUTORS (P) LTD

Published by
ATLANTIC
PUBLISHERS & DISTRIBUTORS (P) LTD
7/22, Ansari Road, Darya Ganj, New Delhi-110002
Phones : +91-11-40775252, 23273880, 23275880, 23280451
Fax : +91-11-23285873
Web : www.atlanticbooks.com
E-mail : orders@atlanticbooks.com

Branch Office
5, Nallathambi Street, Wallajah Road, Chennai-600002
Phones : +91-44-64611085, 32413319
E-mail : chennai@atlanticbooks.com

ISBN 978-81-269-1709-9

Printed in India at Nice Printing Press, A-33/3A, Site-IV, Industrial Area, Sahibabad, Ghaziabad, U.P.

Foreword

'Autism' is a disorder which many people in India are unaware of. The world sees autism as hopeless or impossible condition to mitigate. Parents are often prone to lose hope. The possibilities of medical sciences in helping the autistic children are always unclear. The touch of humanity, sympathy, compassion, etc. are more paramount than the medical cure in minimizing the troubles of autistic children. Nothing is beyond our reach if we honestly believe that we can do it.

Most of the parents do not know that their child is autistic. The parents of all the cases presented in this book are unaware of their children's autistic condition. At this juncture, I appreciate the work taken up by the author and her dedication and commitment to bring awareness in parents about autism and educating them on various methods and techniques available to overcome the difficulties of their autistic children.

This book is useful to gain information and impart training skills to parents and social workers to cope up with autistic children. I am glad to write a foreword for the research work done by I. Victoria Susan and published by the Atlantic Publishers and Distributors (P) Ltd.

Dr. G. Charan Roy
Civil Assistant Surgeon

Preface

The words that the parents of special children often hear more than anyone else are "that's impossible". Autism is such a disorder. It is a complex developmental disability that typically appears during the first three years of a child's life. It is estimated to occur in as many as two to six in thousand individuals.

Many people with autism and their families will cope up well with autism but the emotional impact of autism is often difficult and sometimes devastating, both to the affected people, and their families. In my observation I found that parents are often unaware of their child's autistic condition. They attribute it to mental retardation or some other causes. However, parents learn eagerly the techniques and methods of improving their child's condition when explained to them. The experiences with the parents, teachers, and the autistic children motivated me to publish the work.

This book contains four chapters in which information and case studies of Autism Spectrum Disorders are represented. In the last chapter, methods to cope with autism children are given. I hope that those who read this book will acquire skills to recognize autism in children early, to manage the children with autism and to train and instruct others to get success in the management of children with autism.

I. Victoria Susan

Acknowledgements

This book is the result of the hard work of many well-wishers. I thank the parents and the children who were taken up for this study. I appreciate their cooperation, assistance and encouragement for publication of this book. I am grateful to Mrs. G. Lalitha for her assistance and encouragement all through for production of this book. I thank the managements of Chaitanya Manovikasa Kendram, Chirala and Dakshinya, Guntur for their cooperation and encouragement in my work. I thank Dr. B. Vijay Kumari for her guidance and valuable suggestions.

I. Victoria Susan

Contents

1

Introduction

INTRODUCTION

All children irrespective of cast, creed, religion and disability should get equal opportunity to develop their personality. The child rights and the human rights, across all the governments in the world, are stressing this point. The growth and development of various mental abilities and capacities start right from the birth of an individual. The process of mental growth and development is responsible for the development of an individual's cognitive, mental, intellectual abilities like perception, imagination, sensation, memory, reasoning, understanding, intelligence, generalisation, interpretation, language ability, conceptual ability, problem-solving ability and decision-making ability, etc.

The development of various abilities; the require as adults; proceed simultaneously and continuously from infancy, yet the studies have revealed the possibility of differences in the rate of mental development at various ages. The differences represent either the possibility of greater growth or retarded growth in some aspects, result in exceptional children.

Exceptional children are those that deviate significantly from the normal ones. In other words, children who show a considerable deviation from what is supposed to be average intelligence to their age group are labelled as exceptional children. The deviation may fall on either side and therefore, the exceptional may be significantly below average or significantly above average in various aspects of human growth and development. Such children are exceptionally inferior or superior to the normal children in terms of physical development, mental ability, social behaviour and emotional reactions. They experience a sort of maladjustment in life. They need special care and education for proper adjustment.

One such exceptional quality of children is AUTISM. Autism is a complex developmental disability that typically appears during the first three years of life. It results in neurological disorder that effects the functioning of the brain. Autism and its associated behaviour patterns have been estimated to occur in 2 to 6 in 1,000 individuals. The prevalence of autism is four times more in boys than in girls and knows no racial, ethnic or social boundaries.

In 1943, Leo Kanner first described AUTISM. This perplexing and highly enigmatic disorder is characterised by difficulty in interacting with others normally. They have speech, language and communication impairments. At the same time, most of the individuals with autism have normal physical growth and development.

Autism spectrum disorders are some of the most common developmental disorders which effect one in every 100 school children. Boys are four times more likely to develop autism than girls. The word can be confusing to the individual with autism. They can't understand or acquire the appropriate behaviour to their age.

Many people and their families with autism will cope up well with the additional challenges the autism brings in, but the emotional impact of autism is often difficult and sometimes devastating to the affected people and their families.

Hence, the researcher has taken up the present study on autism. The study has been suitably titled as "AUTISM SPECTRUM DISORDER—A STUDY".

CONCEPTUAL BACKGROUND

Meaning of Autism

Autism spectrum disorder is a general term used to cover a range of difficulties that occur in three main aspects of child development. They are:

1. Communication skills

2. Social skills
3. Life skills

Communication Skills

Communication skills encompass the development of appropriate use of language or speech to communicate, the ability to get information through 'non-verbal' language such as body posture, movement and the ability to communicate information through one's own non-verbal methods.

People with Autism Spectrum Disorder have difficulties in many aspects of communication. Normal children use verbal as well as non-verbal communication and initiate a conversation. The non-verbal communication means the use of the body language like gestures, facial expressions, tone, pitch and intonation of voice to make others know our thoughts, views and feelings. In children the difficulty in communicating with others, is often mistaken as a problem of language and speech. This need not always be the case but it may be Autism Spectrum Disorder.

Social Skills

The healthy infant children are social beings. They gaze at people, turn towards them, turn towards their voices, grasp a finger and even smile. Individuals with autism did not like to interact with others. They avoid eye contact and interaction with others. They seem to prefer being alone. They were often described as aloof. But with the increasing awareness of autism, it is now realised that all children are not aloof. There are some children that respond to others. They do not initiate an interaction or try to initiate an interaction with others, but have odd or socially inappropriate mannerism. The children with autism can't read the facial expressions, gestures and smiles and interpret the feelings of others. This lack of social understanding leads to difficulties in their ability to pay attention to, or understand the emotions of others. The peers and adults that are observing the child with autism may find this odd, naughty or rude mannerism in different situations and move away from that child. The autism children can't predict and understand the actions of others. There is a need to help the child with autism to understand these situations and develop the necessary skills that will facilitate social interaction.

Immature behaviour is found in some children with autism. They lose control and become aggressive when they are frustrated, angry or in a strange environment. In such situations they resort to do any or some of the things like crying, verbal outburst, break things, attack others, bang on their head, pull the hair, bite the nails, etc.

Life Skills

There are individual differences in acquiring the life skills basing on the extent of the autism affects a person. The variation increases basing on the associated impairments and health conditions. Most of the children with autism do have other problems such as mental impairment, tuberculosis, cerebral palsy, down's syndrome, visual impairment, hearing impairment and seizures. Mental impairment is more common than all other disorders. Whatever be the level of Autism Spectrum Disorder, appropriate education will help the child to progress.

Possible Indications of Autism Spectrum Disorder in Early Childhood

1. Poor eye contact.
2. Doesn't smile.
3. Doesn't babble, point or make meaningful gestures by one year.
4. Doesn't speak one word by sixteen months.

In Late Childhood

1. Doesn't know how to play with toys.
2. Lines up toys or other objects excessively.
3. Attach to one particular toy or object.
4. Doesn't respond to name.
5. Some times seems to be hearing impaired.

Possible Difficulties in Autism Spectrum Disorder

- Eating non-edibles (pica).
- Eating certain items only (choosy eating).
- Nutrition deficiency.
- Difficulty in sleeping.
- Insensitivity to pain.
- Susceptibility to allergin.
- Self-injurious behaviour.
- Perseverance (doing things over and over again).
- Inability to accept change.
- Over-activity.
- Severe sensory difficulties.
- Quick upset at certain stimuli.

Possible Strengths in Autism Spectrum Disorder

- Good long-term memory.
- Good music/drawing abilities.
- Performing a learnt task accurately.
- Good at jigsaw puzzles and construction toys.
- Good rote memory.
- Ability to do the same task repeatedly.
- Good at computers, mechanical and electrical equipments.

DEFINITION OF AUTISM

Autism is a pervasive developmental disorder. Children and youth identified as having a pervasive developmental disorder, "are characterised by severe and pervasive impairment in several areas like reciprocal social interaction skills, communication skills along with the presence of stereotyped behaviour, interests, and activities."

—*Diagnostic and Statistical Manual of Mental Disorders*, Fourth Edition

Autism is a complex developmental disability and typically appears during the first three years of life. It is the result of neurological disorder that affects the functioning of the brain. Autism and its associated behaviours have been estimated to occur in as many as 2 to 6 in 1,000 individuals.

—*Autism Society of America Definition of Autism*

Autism is a developmental disability significantly affecting verbal and non-verbal communication and social interaction generally evident before age 3, that adversely affects a child's educational performance. Other characteristics often associated with autism are engagement in repetitive activities and stereotyped movements, resistance to environmental change, or change in daily routines, and unusual responses to sensory experiences. The term does not apply if a child's educational performance is adversely affected primarily, because the child has an emotional disturbance. A child who manifests the characteristics of autism after the said age, could be diagnosed as having "autism" if the criteria above is satisfied (20 U.S.C.S. 1400).

—*Federal Definition of Autism*

KINDS OF AUTISM

There are five types of autism disorders:

(1) Classic Autism
(2) Aspergers Syndrome
(3) Childhood Disintegrative Disorder
(4) Rett Syndrome
(5) Pervasive Developmental Disorder-Not Otherwise Specified

(1) Classic Autism

Classic autism is the second leading childhood developmental disorder and is considered the most severe of all types of autism disorders. They develop language late, or never. People affected with classic autism have difficulties in talking to other people. They lack the feeling of affection or a desire to interact with others. They wish for sameness and routineness. In some, the abnormality of speech makes them mute. They have high levels of visio-spatial skills, but face major learning difficulties in other areas. Symptoms of autism usually appear during the first three years of childhood and will continue throughout life. Autism is a spectrum disorder because the severity, the impairment and the disorder in each of these areas differ from person to person.

(2) Aspergers Syndrome

A person with Aspergers syndrome can exhibit a variety of characteristics and the disorder can range from mild to severe. Children show deficiencies in social skills and have difficulties with transitions or change. They compulsively cling to rituals and any change in their routine can upset them. They have a great difficulty in reading the body language and in determining proper body space. Some children with Aspergers syndrome have low sensitivity to pain and a high sensitivity to bright lights and loud noises. The people suffering from this type of autism disorders have average or above-average intelligence.

(3) Childhood Disintegrative Disorder

Childhood disintegrative disorder includes severe regression in communication skills, social behaviour, and in the development of motor skills. At the beginning these children seem perfectly normal. They start to regress around ages 2-4 years of age. At that time, these children stop socialising, lose potty-training skills, stop playing, lose motor skills and stop making friends.

(4) Rett Syndrome

Rett syndrome is a neurological and developmental disorder that occurs mostly in girls and is marked by poor head growth. Loss of muscle tone is usually the first symptom. Other early symptoms may include problems in crawling or in walking and diminished eye contact. They stop using their hands to do things and often develop stereotyped hand movements, such as wringing, clapping, or patting their hands. The inability to perform motor functions is perhaps the most severe disabling feature of Rett syndrome, interfering with everybody movement, including eye gaze and speech. Infants with Rett syndrome seem to grow and develop normally at first, but then stop developing and even lose skills and abilities.

(5) Pervasive Developmental Disorder-Not Otherwise Specified

This tends to describe people who have many or all of the different types of autism disorders. Children with PDD-NOS either do not fully meet the criteria of symptoms used to diagnose any of the four specific types mentioned above or do not have the degree of impairment described in any of the above four specific types.

DIAGNOSTIC TOOLS AND METHODS

Childhood Autism Rating Scale (CARS)—Schopler *et al.*, 1988

Childhood Autism Rating Scale (CARS) developed by Eric Schopler and his colleagues at division TEACCH, USA, is one of the most popular tools used for the purpose of diagnosis in India as well as all over the world. It can be used with children over 24 months of age. CARS involves an interview with the parents or the child's family members and observation of the child in which fifteen different areas of functioning are assessed. The child's behaviour in each area is related on a seven scale grading and depending upon the overall score of the child, a diagnosis of Autism Spectrum Disorder is given. The rating helps in identifying the differentiations and the degree of autism.

The Autism Diagnostic Interview (ADI)—Le Conter *et al.*, 1989

This as the name suggests is an interview based diagnostic tool, where a structured interview is used to gather information from the parents in all the three areas of impairment. The questions are open ended, reducing the chances of parents providing biased information and the scoring gathered helps in providing a diagnosis on the basis of DSM IV or ICD 10. ADI was developed as a research tool and is widely used for research purposes. Professionals using ADI need to get training and certified in using the tool. This, at present is available only outside India.

The Autism, Diagnostic Observation Schedule (ADOS)—Lord *et al.*, 1989

ADOS uses semi-structural observation environment where the child is observed performing activities in all the three areas of difficulty as well as any additional repetitive behaviour. The child's performance in these activities are given scores, which leads to a diagnosis. Similar to ADI, ADOS also requires training and certification to use and is currently not available in India.

Other Diagnostic Tools and Methods

The Diagnostic Interview for Social and Communication Disorders (DISCD) is again an interview based diagnostic tool. It is supposed to cover the whole autistic spectrum and provide information about the additional conditions such as attention deficit disorder Tourette's syndrome, and obsessive compulsive disorder (Gould, 1988). But its usage is still limited to certain centres only. Several other screening schedules that are available and are being used are Gilliam Autism Rating Scale (GARS), Gilliam Asperger's Disorder Scale (GADS) and Asperger Syndrome Diagnostic Scale (ASDS).

Various Diagnostic tools which are applied to assess cognitive, language and social skills are used in conjunction with the autism specific assessments.

PDD-NOS or a Typical Autism

It is a diagnosis which is used when the child does not show all the features of autism, or the age, at which the difficulties set in is later than 36 months. In spite of the differences all the strategies that are applicable to people with autism are also useful to people with a typical autism.

Childhood Disintegrative Disorder

In this disorder the child seems to develop normally till around 36 months and then there is regression in the areas of speech, communication skills and social skills. The main feature that distinguishes this term is the age of onset. This is not always clear, and depends much on the memory of the families. There is a controversy about the relevance of this term.

Rett's Syndrome

It is basically found in girls. A child with Rett's syndrome would develop normally until around one year to 18 months of age, then the motor skills start to deteriorate rapidly. This affects the child's gait or way of walking and the child starts losing the efficiency in the use of hands and a new way of hand washing/wriggling kind of movement develops. Communication skills also get affected although the interest in interaction is not lost altogether.

Mental/Visual/Hearing Impairment and ASD

In mental impairment, the development of cognitive skills is affected. Thus the child may function below normal, to the appropriate age level. In visual or hearing impairments, the cognitive area need not be affected but the primary difficulty lies in hearing or seeing.

People with severe mental impairments and sensory impairments (vision or hearing) may develop self-stimulatory behaviour like rocking, hand flapping, head shaking. In some cases of mental impairment, communication skills could also be affected leading to limited social skills. The main difference between mental impairment and autism is that while in mental impairment all areas of development are equally affected. In autism, social, communication and imagination skills are the primary areas that get affected.

Dyspraxia/Dyslexia and ASD

Dyslexia is a term used to define children who have specific difficulty in reading, writing and other learning skills. People with dyslexia could have normal intelligence but their difficulty lies in reading and writing that leads to poor academic performance. Dyslexia is usually associated with dyspraxia. In dyspraxia, the ability to co-ordinate the movement of the body is affected, even though there is no identifiable physical handicaps with the limbs of the body. This could affect specific areas such as oral dyspraxia (difficulty in planning and implementing oral movements needed for speech production) to a more generalised motor planning difficulty.

People with high-functioning autism or asperger syndrome usually have difficulties with motor skills and motor planning which are the main features of dyspraxia. Some people with autism also have difficulties with visual and auditory perception like that of some people with dyslexia. It is difficult to distinguish dyslexia from high-functioning autism in younger children, but the difference usually gets more apparent by the time children reach 6-8 years of age. When a differential diagnosis is applied, dyspraxia or dyslexia is found as adding difficulties in some people with Autism Spectrum Disorder.

CHARACTERISTICS OF AUTISM AND MANAGEMENT STRATEGIES

(i) Difficulty in Relating to Others

Characteristics: Children with autism have great difficulty in relating themselves to children around them. However, some do develop closeness with adults who are sensitive to their needs. Some children develop obsessive attachment to certain adults and when separated, suffer from separation anxiety and panic attacks. One prominent characteristic is children with autism do not develop relationships or friendship network with same age children. Since there is no single test for autism, inability to form friendships with classmates and same age children is a definite test.

Strategy: Montessori classrooms, where mixed age group children are assigned to each class, provide a great outlet. Older children could be friends to the children with autism. If this is not possible, pair the child with autism with an older child in the same class.

(ii) Resistance to Change

Characteristics: Normally young children and youth are more pliable and have flexibility to adapt to new situations. But the children with autism are reluctant to change. They derive a lot of comfort in maintaining sameness and sticking to their routine. Children with autism feel comfortable in known predictable settings.

Strategy: Introduce CHANGE as a card, as a part of the daily time table. If the class teacher is absent, a substitute teacher attends the class. If there are any visitors at school or at house, if there are any new activities that have been planned at school or at house, change in his attendants, change of attendant that will pick up the child, shall be informed to the child well in advance before it occurs. Autism child needs more processing time to accept the change.

Normal children like variety. For children with autism variety is not the spice of their life. They experience a great degree of comfort in sameness. Then how to introduce variety? Introduce variety slowly and repeatedly so that they do not get stuck with a particular method or a person or a setting. If a child with autism likes to wear only pink shirt and pink knickers, slowly introduce pink with blue stripes. See that the pink area is more in the beginning and get smaller and smaller gradually. In course of time, if the underwear is pink, the child could be made tolerable in wearing shirts and jeans of different colours. However, respect the child's preference for a particular colour.

(iii) Stereotyped Behaviour

Characteristics: Stereotyped behaviour is defined as that behaviour which is repetitive and does not serve any purpose. It has an important place in autistic child's life.

Dr. Gregory Valcante, Director of the CARD, Centre of University of Florida, had mentioned in a paper on the range of stereotypic behaviours exhibited by children with autism.

Head: Shaking, nodding, tilting head or even standing upside down, hitting head against wall or hitting with hand or head butting others.

Eyes: Poking eyes and there by creating visual stimulation movement, squinting starting at rotating objects, or hand turning in front of the eyes.

Ears: Slapping ears (usually the child might have an ear infection or ear ache), plugging ears (usually the child will be suffering from sensitive hearing and subsequent pain at certain decibels), pulling the ear lobe.

Nose: Sniffing at everything, inserting objects in nose, pulling the nose.

Mouth: Making noises, grunts, squeals, eating or mouthing in non-edible objects, chewing plastic, squishing saliva, gargling water, slapping on mouth or pulling lips or peeling lips.

Skin: Picking on boils, on pimples, pinching and rubbing the skin.

Hands: Hand turning, making clicking sound, clapping, flapping, usually engaging in fine motor activities that are not constructive.

Legs: Walking on tiptoe, shuffling, shaking legs, jumping and climbing on window sills or parapet walls, etc.

Strategy: Children with autism have sensory dysfunction. They could either be hyper sensitive or hypo sensitive to sensory stimuli. If hyper sensitive, the child will avoid a sensation, and if hypo sensitive, the child will seek the same. The child, who closes his ears, is hyper sensitive to certain decibels of sound. If a child is hypo sensitive he would like to produce sound from every toy he plays with or tap a surface. Most of the children with autism seeks movement and they could be hyperactive. The stereotyped behaviour or the repetitive voluntary/involuntary movements serve a purpose to the child of autism. This aspect should be managed with a lot of care.

(iv) Echolalia

Echolalia means repetition of words, phrases or sentences just heard by the child. Echolalia is of two kinds. They are immediate and delayed. The child will repeat immediately the pleasing things uttered by elders like "shall we go out?" They will repeat after a gap of sometime the words of reprimands, scoldings, and shoutings at them by the elders. They do it by talking aloud by themselves like “don’t talk, be quiet” etc.

Researchers who started to work with children with autism considered echolalia as unwanted verbal behaviour, something that interferes with learning. The children were conditioned to stop it by giving a slap or loud “Don’t Echo” or “No” commands (Lovaas, 1987). Extinguishing the behaviour was the main objective of the intervention. Dr. Prizant and Whetherby, after extensive research, found out that children with autism learnt language in a very unconventional manner (Unconventional Verbal Behaviour—UVB) and that they tended to memorise whole chunks of verbal responses as un-analysed phrases. These responses served all the functions of normal speech (Whetherby, 1986) such as:

- Turn taking
- Yes answer
- Questions
- Requests
- Reprimands
- Self-regulation

Thus, echolalia serves a purpose for the child. Echo response may be unconventional verbal behaviour, but that is the only strategy the child has (Prizant & Duchan, 1981). Do not slap the child or tell the child to shut up; the child may become non-verbal due to the negative conditioning. Instead give the correct response. If the communicative intent is expression of anxiety or panic attack (test situation, unfamiliar people, crowd) you can say “afraid”, “itisOK” (as one word). Sometimes children with autism picks up whole phrases from Cartoon shows or TV shows and insert them in a situation. Parents can often tell others, the meaning of the phrases and the context in which the child heard the phrases. Echolalia is also another form of self talk that even persons without autism exhibit. Talking to self, helps a person to stay alert, be motivated and to stay calm. If the behaviour calls attention to the child’s autism, you may instruct the child to go to a room and talk but not in the company. This behaviour can't be extinguished completely.

(v) Lectoralness of Language

Children with autism often do not understand jokes, pun or subtle expressions. They tend to take things literally. Do not be sarcastic or use idiomatic verbal expression with autism children as they will miss the communicative intent. Be very direct, when you talk to them.

(vi) Attachment to Objects

It is common to all children to get attached to objects. Every one will have their own favourite dress, colour, chair or bed, etc. and so do children with autism get attached to certain things. Uninterrupted daily routine gives a feeling of happiness to children of autism.

Strategy: If an autistic child is fond of an object or thing do not separate the object or thing from the child. The object provides a sense of sameness and comfort to the child in unfamiliar or stressful situations.

The object could be a strip of paper, deck, cards, a string or a blue block. The child keeps the object in unfamiliar settings as it provides security. However, if it bothers you too much, then you may start reducing the time the child keeps the object or the size of it during break time while the child is not playing with it.

A strip should suffice, instead of a whole blanket. Sensory toys are available in the market which can act as fidget toys. Look for novel and appropriate toys you can provide while travelling or when the child is needed to sit quiet for extended period of time.

(vii) Obsessive Compulsive Behaviour

Usually the special interest of the child will become evident by age three. Following the ritual or a set pattern gives comfort to the child. Find out how else you can provide a sense of security. Do not make a big issue of it. If you extinguish the behaviour prematurely, another one will take its place as you have not addressed the basic needs like stress relief, sensory pleasure, communicative interest of the child. Some of the behaviours exhibited by them are:

- Counting steps, or squares on the floor
- Always holding a favourite toy
- Same sequence of steps for certain daily activities like sleeping, toileting
- Smelling all surfaces
- Licking all objects
- Speaking out certain disturbed thought processes

Pharmacotherapy is often tried for severe Obsessive Compulsive Disorders (OCD) if the disorder interferes with the child's ability to cope with activities of daily living. However, the other issues like behaviour management, cognitive training, etc., need to be addressed, alongside. Simple pill popping (using medicine) will not help.

(viii) Eating, Elimination and Sleep Problems

All the three problems could be inter-related. If the child is not eating right, most probably the child is not getting adequate fibre and is constipated. This can interfere with elimination and sleep.

Strategy: Physical activity can be introduced during the day, and make sure that the child goes to play in the outdoors in the evening sun. Yoga could be tried. Check whether the child is hyperactive. Dietary intervention can also be tried. Toilet training is a very important issue by itself. Unless the child eats at set times everyday the need to eliminate cannot be pinpointed. Dinner should be before 8 p.m. So that morning hours can be devoted to toilet training. In some houses, the child is fed on demand and is snacking right through the day and night. The habit is not conducive to toilet training. Families need to change their lifestyle to make the child toilet trained.

(ix) Hyperactivity and Problems with Attention

Hyperactivity manifests quiet early; child may be colicky, difficult to fall asleep or stay awake, can't sleep for more than 2-3 hours, poor or picky eaten, does not soothe easily.

Strategy: Ayurvedic treatment is beneficial. Encouraging results were got from Ayurveda treatment to the children suffering from ASD. It is relevant here because a hyperactive child is able to follow directions and can sit on a seat for a stipulated time. Then the child will be able to adjust to regular classroom sitting.

It is better to incorporate movement, than to retrain the child. Junk food and excessive sugar can be avoided. Occupational therapy suggested allopathic drugs like Ritalin and Screnance. They are usually prescribed to counteract hyperactivity. Judith Blustone, a person with Asperger's syndrome, suggests that those with hyperactivity should wear anklets made of copper or silver to earthen the extra electrical impulses. The Indian custom of children wearing silver anklets might have been originated from such belief.

(x) Attention

Keeping attention in a problem to the children with ASD. They shift attention from one activity to other activity very quickly. The span of attention is very short. Even the children under three years show extremely long attention span in doing favourite activities. So the problem is not with attending to a task but focussing on relevant visual stimuli.

There are two types of Attention:

(1) Over-selectivity

(2) Under-selectivity

Over-selectivity of attention is a common characteristic with children with autism. Literally they mistake the 'tree for the woods'. Any tiny logo or icon catch the eye of the child with autism and rest of the visual stimulus is ignored. It is very common to see children with autism play with a wheel of a toy car rather than the toy car.

Strategy: While presenting an activity, make sure that there is visual clarity. The child will take the presented activities as a whole in a tray. Highlighting can orient the child to the relevant facts.

(xi) Problem with Hyperacusis and Auditory Processing

Majority of children with autism suffer from a painful condition called Hyperacusis. They perceive sounds in a magnified or distorted way and often have painful hearing to certain decibels. They will cover their ears, rock or hum to ease the pain. High pitched voices like children screaming, dogs barking, thunder or Diwali crackers cause a severe stress to them. In fact, they hear those sounds that are not normally audible to human ears, resulting in pain and stress. They are particularly sensitive to human voices, but can tolerate those that come through mike, audio cassettes or TV/Radio. Some children resort to humming sound to block painful noises. With such children, you should talk less and show more concern.

Strategy: Speak to them in a low voice. Mothers, therapists, and teachers need to train their voices, especially when they are angry. You can say 'mother is angry' or 'teacher is angry' in an even voice. In short 'switch off affect' as Dr. Asperger advised teachers, keep the face neutral.

Some behaviour problems may have underlying hyperacusis issue resulting in the child becoming aggressive or unmanageable. Auditory Integration Therapy is a mechanically assisted therapy that helps to ease the pain experienced by children with autism. Through not documented through empirical evidence, anecdotal reports do point to the fact that when verbal commands are processed well the child is able to respond better and generally shows improved academic achievement.

(xii) Problems with Generalisation

This had been one of the drawbacks of many programmes developed for students with autism until the late eighties. They are unable to generalise or transfer a concept learnt in one situation to another. Hence, a child toilet trained at home may not use the same facility at school.

Strategy: Teachers and parents need to communicate regularly and clearly. Concepts taught at school should have a real life focus. Family members of children with autism shall take up the tasks. The mother will help with toileting, father will take them out, grandmother will cook favourite food and grandfather will play. All the activities should be interchanged so that when a particular member is not available others can take on the role. The setting needs to be varied so that a phrase like PUSH can mean:

- Push button—switch on the light
- Push swing—give a push to the swing
- Push door—to open the door
- Push cycle—for another child
- Push merry—go—round—for children seated
- Don't push—not to push.

(xiii) Poor Pretend Play and Imagination

The children of autism are poor in pretend play and imagination. The other two deficiencies are communication skills and social skills. This is a very important aspect of diagnosis and intervention. Improvement in this one area alone will have a domine effect and results in lessened autism quotient.

Strategy: Children with autism usually play at the exploratory stage, mounting, sounding or feeling toys. They seem to get 'stuck' at a stage. The parents or the teachers can help them get unstuck by teaching pretend and symbolic play. Some children possess very fantastic pretend play ability. In some autism children, pretend play and language development will be on par with normal children. The very innovative teachers can actually do the impossible things in equating the children of ASD. In the process of getting the students confirm the presence of Autism Spectrum Disorder, the teachers should allow the child to express his originality.

Every mother of autism child was asked to collect a sample of 100 utterances of spontaneous communication of her child to check the index of productive syntax. When the utterances were assessed, I found that the child had superior language skills of pretend play and imagination. Normal methods of gathering the data would not have yielded such results as the child did not talk to strangers.

(xiv) Emotions

Teach children to identify the emotions like happy, sad, angry and fear. Identify an emotion, not just by pointing to happy and sad faces but understand the inner state. Understand what contributes to that particular emotion and how to express the same. Teach when the child is experiencing the emotion.

(xv) Poor Organisation and Planning

Children with autism have problems with praxis, copying movements, combining gross and fine motor movements, attempting new movements during physical exercises, etc. Motor movement development involves the control of limbs. Fine motor movement are done by hands, arms and fingers. Gross motor movements are done by legs and feet. All these learning process result from the experiences.

INTERVENTIONS AND TREATMENTS

Interventions and treatments are grouped into five broad categories:

(1) Interpersonal relationship interventions and treatments
(2) Skill-based inventions and treatments
(3) Cognitive interventions and treatments
(4) Physiological/biological/neurological interventions and treatments
(5) Other interventions and treatments.

They are also grouped as:

(1) Science based practices

(2) Promising practice

(3) Limited supporting information practices

(1) Science based practices: Science based practices are those that have significant and convincing empirical efficacy, supported by scientific data.

(2) Promising practices: The promising practice refer to methods that appear to have efficacy and utility with individuals with ASD, even though the intervention requires additional scientific support to be considered as science based method.

(3) Limited supporting information practices: They are used to describe interventions and treatments for which there is little or no scientific evidence of utility. These methods are available to use on individuals with ASD, although it is not clear whether they have utility and efficacy.

	Interpersonal relationship interventions & treatments	Skill Based interventions and treatments	Cognitive interventions and treatments	Physiological/ Biological / Neurological interventions and treatments	Other interventions and treatments
Scientifically based practice		Applied Behaviour Analysis (ABA) Disoute Trial Teaching (DTT) Pivotal Response Training (PRT)	Learning experience. An alternative programme for preschoolars and parents (Leap)		
Promising Practice	Play-Oriented Strategies	Assistive Technology Augmentative Alternative Communication (AAC) Incidental Teaching Joint Action Routines (JARS) Picture Exchange Communication System (PECS) Structured Teaching (TEACCH)	Cognitive Behavioural Modification Cognitive Learning Strategies Social Decision-Making Strategies Social stories	Pharmacology Sensory Integration (SI)	
Limited Supporting Information for Practice	Gentle Teaching Option Method (Son-Rise Program) Floor Time	Fast For Word van Dijk Curricular Approach	Cartooning Cognitive Scripts Power Cards	Auditory Integration Training (AIT) Megavitamin Therapy Scotopic Sensitivity	Art Therapy Candida: Austism Connection Feingold Diet, Herb, Mineral, and other

	Pet/Animal Therapy Relationship Development Intervention (RDI)			Syndrome (SSS): Irlen Lenses	supplements Gluten-Casein Intolerance Mercury: Vaccinations and Autism Music Therapy
Not Recommended	Holding Therapy	Facilitated Communication (FC)			

CONCEPTUAL MODEL

Autism Spectrum Disorder

Individual characteristics

(1) Family background
(2) Genetic factors
(3) Health condition

General characteristics

(a) Communication skills
(b) Social skills
(c) Life skills

2

Review of Related Literature

INTRODUCTION

Research in any field is fruitful only when the researcher is aware of the past studies. Research is a continuous process. A review of related literature is necessary for every research study. The required insight into the present problem can be developed as a result of previous research.

The knowledge of the previous research helps to view the problem with precision and accuracy. The hypothesis can be arrived at on the basis of theoretical background. It provides the background for selection of research procedures, the comparison of data and interpretation of results. This will help in precision and economy. It helps to avoid the pitfalls by earlier researchers.

Very few researches are available on Autism Spectrum Disorder. Based on first chapter, and on the conceptual background of the Autistic children, the investigator would like to have some knowledge about the problem of Autistic children to carry out the study. The review of the previous studies is classified as Foreign studies and Indian studies.

RESEARCH ON AUTISM SPECTRUM DISORDER

Foreign Studies

(1) ***Title: Genetics of Autism Clinical Research Project***

Researcher: Department of Human Genetics, Emory University (2009)

Abstract

The purpose of this research project is to learn more about genetic causes of autism in families that have one of the children affected by a known Autism Spectrum Disorder (ASD). Families have an opportunity to contribute to the knowledge of ASDs by participating voluntarily in diagnostic assessment of the child with ASD. The parents answer the interviews, complete the questionnaires, tell about family members, and give a blood sample. They determine the eligibility of a family for selection for study after a telephonic interview.

The selected family shall have one child in the age group of 4-17 years with a diagnosed ASD, along with a sibling who has no ASD. Both the biological parents shall accept to participate. At least one sibling in the age group of 4-17 shall be available to participate. The families with no siblings or siblings who are too young to participate are not accepted. No other children in the family shall have ASD. All the members of the participating family must express their willingness to give a blood sample.

The evaluation of the child with an ASD, includes information about the child's diagnosis, cognition and adaptive behaviour and recommendations for intervention. The assessment team typically consists of psychologists, developmental paediatricians and geneticists. The family will receive a research summary of the results at no cost.

(2) *Title: Understanding the Symbolic Nature of Pictures in Children with Autism*

Researcher: KRISTEN Mc FEE
A trainee with the CIAR-NAAR
Inter-Institute ASD strategic trainer

Abstract

Symbolic understanding or the ability to recognise and use symbols in a variety of situations, is a skill which emerge in the first few years of life and is the basis for a number of human characteristics such as language, reading and pretend play. Children today obtain knowledge through the use of a variety of symbols such as books, television and computers as well as other forms of symbolic media including pictures and scale-models. The previous research has shown that developing children between 2.5 years and 3.5 years of age are able to use pictures and scale-models effectively. There is no research examining the ability of individuals with autism to recognise and use pictures, symbols in different situations.

The use of "Hide and Seek" game, where children were asked to find a hidden toy in a doll house with the help of a picture that depicts the hiding location. Normal children were able to identify it easily. The researcher attempted to study whether the children with autism were able to understand the picture representing the actual object, and use the information to organise their searching behaviour and succeed in finding the actual object.

The researcher found that children with autism that were learning verbal skills over 36 months were successful in locating the hidden objects, using the picture as an aid. They demonstrated proficiency in understanding the symbols. The autism children that were learning verbal skills for less than 30 months could not locate the hidden object. The researcher proposes to develop overall social communicative abilities, effective alternative communication systems the ways to use symbols in teaching and therapeutic intervention if necessary, to improve the symbolic understanding in autism children and to promote the use of symbols by autistic children.

(3) *Title: Can Tutors Teach Children with Autism, Through Self-Instruction*

Researcher: LINDSAY ARNAL
A trainee with the UHR-NAAR
Inter-Institute ASD strategic trainee

Abstract

Several Canadian provinces are funding early intensive behavioural intervention programmes for children with autism spectrum disorders. This has created a demand for well-trained tutors to provide one-to-one training for the children. An effective method to prepare tutors is needed. The present research addresses this need. The researcher worked with Dr. Garry Martin and C.T. Yu and other graduation students at the Mahitoba University and at the St. Mount Research Centre. The present study evaluated, whether University students of autism can learn by self-instruction? The teaching strategy is through intervention programmes based on applied behaviour analysis. The results are highly promising. The refinements of the self-instructional packages and additional studies are currently under way.

(4) *Title: Participation of Children with and without Disabilities in Social—Recreational and Leisure Activities*

Researcher: ABBIE SOLISH

Abstract

In this research the Typically Developing (TD) children that are neither autistic nor intellectually disable, are compared with the children diagnosed with Autism Spectrum Disorder (ASD) and with the children diagnosed with Intellectual Disability (ID) in respect of their participation in social, recreational and leisure activities.

The researcher has explored certain activities for 185 children to participate. The parents of the children were asked to monitor their own child's performance, and record it in the given questionnaire. Out of 185 children,

(1) 90 children are TD

(2) 65 children are ASD

(3) 30 children are ID

The parents recorded the activities of their child over the 34 items of the questionnaire. The parents completed the questionnaire that measures their own child's participation in the following activities.

(1) Social activities

(2) Recreational activities

(3) Leisure activities

The parents recorded the activities of their children over the 34 items in the questionnaire. The parents provided the information about the friendship of their children.

The participation of TD children in social and recreational activities is more than that of the children with ASD or ID.

(1) The percentage of TD children, participated in social and recreational activities is high when compared to their peers of ASD and ID. Very few students of TD participated in leisure activities.

(2) Some differences emerged between the ASD and ID groups although they are similar in many ways. The children with ASD participated in more leisure activities with adults than the children with ID. Furthermore, the children with ASD participated in fewer recreational activities with peers than the children with ID.

(3) TD children have more mutual friends along with some best friends than the children with ASD or ID.

(4) The children with ID have more mutual friends along with some best friends than the children with ASD.

Many children with disabilities have friends and are participating in activities.

The research highlighted how children with disabilities could make few friendships than their TD peers. It is observed that 50 per cent of the children with ASD and 80 per cent of the children with ID in this study had at least one mutual friend. Furthermore, the activity participation of the students is not identical across groups. It is recognised that many children with disabilities engage in community activities with the peers.

(5) *Evidence of Major Environmental Trigger for Autism*

Researcher: MICHAEL WALDMAN
Johnson Graduate School of Management
at Cornell University, Ithaca (2008)

Abstract

This analysis is an important step towards identifying a specific environmental trigger, or triggers for Autism. Many autism experts believe that the disorder is triggered by the combination of an environmental and genetic predisposition. The previous literature provides few clues on identifying environmental triggers.

This research attempts to investigate what is the specific trigger that is causing Autism Spectrum Disorder. Wallman, a Professor of Management and Economics, and the Co-author Syan Nicholson, Ph.D. of the College of Human Ecology at Cornels, adds, "They have looked at the hypothesis using three different statistical approaches and in each case, we found strong evidence consistent with hypothesis."

John Williams, Ph.D. of the Department of Child and Adolescent Psychiatry at the Philadelphia-based Children's Hospital of Pennsylvania also contributed to the study. In regard to the team's findings, he says that there is a provocative data that will generate a lot of discussion in the clinician and patient communities. The researchers discussed several possible environmental triggers of Autism. They are early childhood excess viewing of television and video, the increased rate of vitamin D deficiency, and an increased exposure to chemicals used in household cleaners as children who spend more time indoors would likely experience. The research team plans to conduct further statistical studies aimed at identifying which of these possibilities are actual triggers for autism.

The study analysed data from different schools across various counties in the States of California, Oregon and Washington about the prevalence of Autism Spectrum Disorder. The analysis showed that there is positive relationship with the county's annual perception and early exposure to more precipitation prior to the age of 3 years. The findings based on statistical estimate suggest that as many as 30 per cent or more of autism diagnosis is due to an environmental trigger or triggers related to levels of precipitation where the children live. The researcher felt that further study is required on the possible environmental triggers discussed in this study.

Indian Studies

(1) *Title: Cognitive Competence in Infancy*

Researcher: ANANDA LAXMY, S.
Department of Child Development Lady Irwin College, New Delhi (1982)

Abstract

The main objective of the study is to assess the maternal components of affiliation and cognitive stimulation and their effects on the development of the infants. The hypotheses formulated are:

(1) the infant's motor development is related to his health and nutritional status,

(2) the infant's cognitive development is related to his health and nutritional status,

(3) the infant's cognitive and motor development are related to the kind of mother-infant interaction.

Findings

1. For Psychomotor Development Index (PDI) in various age groups, the 't' values between lower and upper, and between lower-middle and upper socio-economic levels are significant for all age groups expect for the youngest age group.
2. Children from the upper socio-economic level in the 18-21, and 21-25 months age groups performed significantly better on MDI (Mental Development Index) than their counterparts in the lower-middle and low socio-economic levels.
3. Cognitive development in infancy as indicated by MDI is not related to nutritional status.
4. The correlation between maternal cognitive stimulation and the child's performance on the mental scale is significant.
5. The results of the follow up study indicated that most of the infants declined in their developmental indices (PDI and MDI).

(2) *Title: Learning Disabilities of Primary School Children*

Researcher: DESAI, K.G.
Department of Education Gujarat
University (1985)

Abstract

The main objectives of the investigation are:

(1) to study different types of learning disabilities commonly found in grade IV children in Ahmedabad city,

(2) to investigate their probable cases, and

(3) to devise and try out remedies for correcting those learning disabilities.

The hypotheses tested are:

(1) Parental disregard of the studies of their children is a major factor affecting disabilities in learning.

(2) Apathy of teachers on certain children destroys in them the interest to learn.

(3) Low intelligence of some pupils is the case of disability of learning language and arithmetic.

Findings

(1) The most potent cause of learning disability is poverty.

(2) The second cause of the malady is the apathy of teachers to their duties in school.

(3) The third cause of learning disability is the abolition of examinations from standards I and II in the schools of Gujarat.

(4) Low intelligence is also a cause of the malady.

(3) *Title: A Study of Influence of Mother's Personality on Child's Personality*

Researcher: BARLINGE, M.K.
Department of Psychology
Nag. University (1977)

Abstract

The investigation is aimed at studying the relationship between certain personality characteristics of mothers and those of their children.

Of the twenty-six variables selected for the study of mothers, sixteen were the personality dimensions of Cattell and ten were different child-rearing practices followed by mothers. Twelve were comprehensive personality dimensions corresponding closely to those of mothers, ten were related to children's perception of mother's child-rearing behaviour and four were common reaction tendencies observed in children.

Findings

The comparison of mother's factor scores and children's original scores revealed that:

(1) The children of emotionally balanced mothers tended to be less hostile than those of mothers of emotional imbalance.

(2) The children of prudent mothers were less negativistic and less hostile to parents than those of non-prudent mothers.

(3) The children of sanguine mothers appeared to be relaxed where as those of less sanguine mothers tended to be tense.

(4) The children of anxious possessive mothers tended to be tense negativistic and hostile towards parents.

(5) The negativism and hostility to parents were always found in children if their mothers had an unhealthy personality and if they followed undesirable child-rearing practices. It was concluded that good child-rearing practices followed by mothers were more important than the personality traits possessed by them.

(4) *Title: Patterns of Psychological Problem of Children of 5-13 years—Their Etiology and Symptomology*

Researcher: KARLA, N.
Department of Psychology
Agra University (1979)

Abstract

The research attempts to study the behaviour problem of children with a view to understand behaviour disorders with respect to their social background.

The following hypotheses were formulated:

(1) Faulty rearing practices were likely to cause deviation in the behavioural pattern of the child.

(2) An emotionally deprived child was prone to behavioural problems.

(3) Social and economic impoverishment may result in deviant behaviour.

(4) Organic deficiencies may lead to abnormal behaviour.

(5) Age, sex and birth order as well as the family size and structure may influence behaviour.

Findings

(1) Faulty rearing practices resulted in habit disorders, speech defects, personality problems, sleep defects and psychosomatic problems.

(2) Emotional deprivation on the part of the parents led to the problems of personality, habit and anxiety state and, to a lesser extent, scholastic backwardness, psycho-somatic problems and speech defects.

(3) Socio-economic deficiencies of the parents mainly resulted in the problems of habit and sleep rather than other behavioural problems.

(4) Organic deficiencies led to various behavioural problems like scholastic backwardness, habit disorders, speech defeats, feeding problems and anti-social activities.

(5) Birth order, family size and structure, SES and parents education did not play a significant role in causing behavioural problems.

(6) One cause like over protection could lead to enuresis and delayed speech development.

(5) *Title: Special Play Session—A Play-way Method to Help Children with Special Needs*

Researcher: MALLYA, I.P.
Department of Child Development
MSU (1982)

Abstract

The main objectives of the study are:

(1) To compile the case studies to understand the children with special needs through special play sessions.

(2) To understand the nature of special needs.

(3) To understand the behaviour of children with special needs.

(4) To share with some other teachers for integrating the special play sessions in the regular nursery school programme.

(5) To understand the values and functions of special play sessions.

Findings

From the case studies, it is felt that

(a) The child should be accepted as he/she is.

(b) A permissive atmosphere should be created for the child when he plays.

(c) The child should be allowed to set his own place.

(d) Warmth and friendliness should be reflected in the relationship with the child.

(1) The findings of the case studies demonstrated the fact that the class teacher could help the children with special needs if they have some knowledge of individual differences in children, some observation and handling skills, and an insight into children's behaviour.

(2) Based on the findings of the study, an orientation programme for teachers working with children of special needs was worked out.

Part-I → consisted of "Guidelines for the class teachers for developing skills in children" with three modules.

(1) The Identification stage

(2) The Helping stage

(3) The Adjustment stage

Part-II → consisted of "Guidelines for conducting group play sessions."

SUMMARY

A brief summary of the above research studies indicates that:

- The typically developing children between 2.5 and 3.5 years of age are able to use pictures and scale-models effectively.
- The children with autism understood that the picture represented an actual object.
- The children with Autism Spectrum Disorder participated in social activities along with adults.
- The correlation between maternal cognitive stimulation and the child's performance on the mental scale was significant.
- The children of over possessive mothers tended to be tense negativistic and hostile towards parents.

PERCEPTION OF GAPS AND LINKAGE TO THE PRESENT STUDY

Many research studies have been done to find the genetical reasons for autism and also the reasons for their typical behaviour. Very few studies are done especially in India about learning practices and skills for the development of autistic children. The present study has focussed on the in-depth study of each case and to suggest suitable remedial measures to develop learning skills in autistic children.

3

Research Procedure

INTRODUCTION

> If one wants to solve a problem, one must generally know what the problem is. It can be said that a large part of the problem lies in knowing what one is trying to do.
>
> —Kerlinger

The information of a research problem is the first and most important step of the research process. It is like the identification of a destination before undertaking a journey. As in the case of absence of a destination, it is impossible to identify the shortest route. Similarly in the absence of a clear research problem, a precise and economical plan is impossible. A research problem is like the foundation of a building. The type and design of the building is dependent upon the foundation. If the foundation is well designed and strong, one can expect the building to be the same. The research problem serves as the foundation of a research study.

This chapter is primarily concerned with procedure of research adopted in this study, the operational definitions, the criteria and the techniques adopted for selecting the sample, the hypothesis formulated and the procedures of research tool designed are discussed.

STATEMENT OF THE PROBLEM

Autism Spectrum Disorders—A Study

Operational Definitions

Federal Definition of Autism

Autism means a developmental disability significantly affecting verbal communication, non-verbal communication and social interaction, generally evident before the child attains the age 3, that adversely affects a child's educational performance.

Objectives

(1) To identify six cases of the students with autism.

(2) To make an indepth study of each case and find out the reasons and the causes for their Autism Spectrum Disorder.

(3) To identify the specific symptoms of each case and to suggest suitable, remedial therapies, treatments and interventions.

(4) To identify the common symptoms of all the cases.

(5) To suggest general remedial therapies, treatments and interventions.

Hypotheses

The case with autism shows characteristics like:

(1) Poor eye contact

(2) Doesn't smile

(3) Doesn't make meaningful gestures

(3) Difficulty in eating, elimination and sleep problems

(4) Not playing with age peers

(5) Appear deaf

(6) Spinning or toe walking

(7) Show interest in objects than humans

(8) Flopping hands

(9) Prone to tantrums.

Method

For the present study the researcher has taken six children, showing the symptoms of autism for an indepth study. The researcher explores the internal and external causes of their behaviour and tries to help the children, the parents and the teachers about various therapies and treatments available to them. Hence, the case study method was adopted in the present study.

Sample

Six children showing symptoms of autism were selected from psychological institutions in Guntur and Prakasam Districts.

Tools

(1) Questionnaire,

(2) Semi-structured interviews, and

(3) Observations were used as tools to study the present problem.

Case Study Questionnaire

A case study questionnaire was prepared by the Researcher himself consisting of following areas:

(1) Family background and history.

(2) Views of parents and teachers.

(3) Family health and genetic factors.

(4) General characteristics:

(a) Communication skills,

(b) Social skills, and

(c) Life skills.

Semi-structured Interview

Questions were framed for semi-structured interview to know about their emotional behaviour, social behaviour and other school activities.

Observations

The researcher personally observed the cases for a period of 8 months by taking periodic visits to their homes. The researcher gathered a lot of information about their activities, their likes, their dislikes, their behaviour and their interaction with others.

SCHEME OF ANALYSIS

Both quantitative and qualitative methods were used to analyse the data.

4

Analysis, Interpretation, Suggestions and Conclusion

INTRODUCTION

Analysis is a process of interpreting and drawing conclusions from the gathered data. The collected data is broken into smaller units and rearranged in new combinations to discover new facts and relationships. Every effort has been made to study the data from as many angles as possible to find out new and newer facts.

The Head of the Institution

The researcher, as a first step consulted the heads of the rehabilitation institutes like Chaitanya Manovikasa Kendram, Chirala, Dakshinya, Guntur and enquired about the various social and emotional characteristics of the children. The cases of autistic similarity were identified. Further in-depth study was conducted with the consultation of the parents and the doctors to identify the presence of autism, the causes of autism and to suggest suitable remedial therapies, treatments and interventions to help the child.

Parents Report

In all cases, the parents of the identified cases are interviewed with regard to their child's Autism Spectrum Disorder.

Teachers Report

The teachers of the concerned students were also enquired about their behaviour and speed of learning in classroom.

Interview

The parents, the teachers, the peer group and the neighbours are interviewed to find out the signs of autism in the child along with the degree of autism.

Observation

The researcher himself personally observed the students of autistic tendency for a couple of days in various aspects. The researcher observed their communication skills, social skills, life skills, etc. The researcher enquired about the family history of the case and gathered data on health condition of the case. The researcher also gathered information about the emotional behaviour, social behaviour and health of the selected child.

Basing on all the above conditions, six students, with confirmed autism, were taken up for in-depth study.

Children who are autistic are identified from the observations of the concerned parents, teachers, heads of the institutions and finally from the doctors.

CASE NO. 1: R. BHANU GANESH

Bhanu Ganesh's parents say that their son was normal in the beginning but later when he was three years old, he appeared to be deaf. They took him to doctors for complete diagnosis. After brain scanning, speech and audibility tests, neurological tests, etc., the doctors confirmed that the child has mild symptoms of Autism Spectrum Disorder.

Bhanu Ganesh, who is now 4 years old, recently joined in a school. The teacher too confirmed about his stereotyped autistic behaviour like toe walking, appearing to be deaf and elimination problems.

The investigator personally observed the child for few weeks and listed out all the symptoms of autism, he has shown during this period. After making a clear study of the case, the boy was selected for in-depth study.

Personal Data of the Child

Name	:	Ravvarapu Bhanu Ganesh
Age	:	4 years
Sex	:	Male
Order of Birth	:	First
Date of Birth	:	12-02-2006
School	:	Chaitanya Manovikasa Kendram, Chirala
Year of study	:	2010 (just joined)
Caste	:	O.C.
Religion	:	Hindu
Mother Tongue	:	Telugu
Place of Birth	:	Narasaraopet
Father's Name	:	Ravvarapu Madhu Prabhakar
Age	:	43 years
Occupation	:	Business
Mother's Name	:	Goli Lalitha Kumari
Age	:	40 years
Occupation	:	Lecturer
Economic and Social Status	:	Middle Class
Type of House	:	Own tiled house with medium ventilators

Family Background

Ganesh's parents are graduates and well educated. They are very cooperative and are able to understand the sensitive condition of their child. They are of a middle class family and take good care of their children. Younger daughter Leela Greeshma is very active and normal. They have good relationships with their neighbours. Though both the parents are employed they spend good time with their children.

Genetic Factors

At the time of pregnancy, in the eighth month, Bhanu Ganesh's mother was diagnosed as having heavy placenta water, because of which the child's brain is filled with 14 per cent water. Both the parents come from different family backgrounds and they are not closely related. They don't have any confirmed genetic diseases. They are not suffering from diabetes or hypertension. They are healthy and normal. Their daughter is healthy and normal. His maternal uncle has some mild features of autism.

Health Condition of the Case

Bhanu Ganesh is a healthy boy. He has no fits. He doesn't like to speak. If he is interested in any work he calls out his father (or) sister. He sleeps very lately, almost at 12.00 in the night. He has a healthy body with a delicate skin. His eye ball is black and has black hair. He has good teeth but he is reluctant to brush his teeth and it is almost like waging a war for the parents to make him brush his teeth. He is strong and tough as a result of which he constantly climbs up the chairs, falls down and gets hurt.

Communication Skills

Bhanu Ganesh suffers from speech problems, but his memory span is very high. He hears the "owl music" in Jetix his favourite channel in T.V., even from a far distance and quickly runs to the T.V. room and watches the show by flopping his hands.

He cannot read and write. He cannot write even the alphabet. He is poor in learning from pictures and flash cards. He is not able to tell or write his name. His teacher maintains a happy relationship with him. They give full support to the child. He cannot recognise the moods of the teacher whether the teacher is angry, tired, sad or happy. He is very much interested in playing carroms and running. He is also interested in playing with water.

Social Skills

Bhanu Ganesh likes to play with his mother, father, sister and grandmother. But he never likes to mix with strangers or other relatives. He moves to neighbouring houses constantly but never meets people there. When the gate is open he immediately utilises the opportunity and runs out of the house. Guarding him from going out of the house has become a task to the parents. He likes to play with a very young neighbouring kid. He always does whatever the kid tells him to do. He likes to attend parties and functions but never likes to meet people there. He simply enjoys his presence in parties. He likes to watch advertisements in T.V. He sits as close as possible to the T.V. while watching. He specially enjoys "owl" music in Jetix channel.

Life Skills

Bhanu Ganesh is very selective in his food. He won't take food if the items are not of his choice. Sometimes he continues it even for the whole day. He takes milk only with a feeding bottle otherwise he won't drink milk. They could make him drink milk with a glass by giving him a lot of pressure.

He will not inform about toilet needs but whenever he feels so, he himself will go out and finish his toilet needs. He will never inform anybody that he has gone for toilet and move around without getting cleaned. He likes junk food. If he feels hungry, he will bring a plate from kitchen and shows it to her mother. If nobody responds to him, he himself will reach the almirah by dragging a chair; put the items in the plate sits down to eat them. He shows a glass to indicate that he is thirsty. He is very much attached to objects. He will never give to others any object in his hand. If anybody has an object which he likes he tries to grab the object from that person, sometimes he even tries to grab them by force.

Brief Sketch of R. BHANU GANESH (Case 1)

Causes	Symptoms
1) Bhanu Ganesh's mother has excess placenta water in pregnancy.	1) Appears to be deaf
2) He was detected with 14% more water in brain.	2) Do not play with peer group
3) He is attached more to his grandparents and spends more time with them.	3) Do not respond to verbal sounds
4) The parents could not spend more time with the child, as both are employed and busy.	4) Do not sit at one place
	5) Resort to spin and the toe walking
	6) Flop hands
	7) Depend on others for daily routine work like personal cleanliness, eating, drinking, etc.

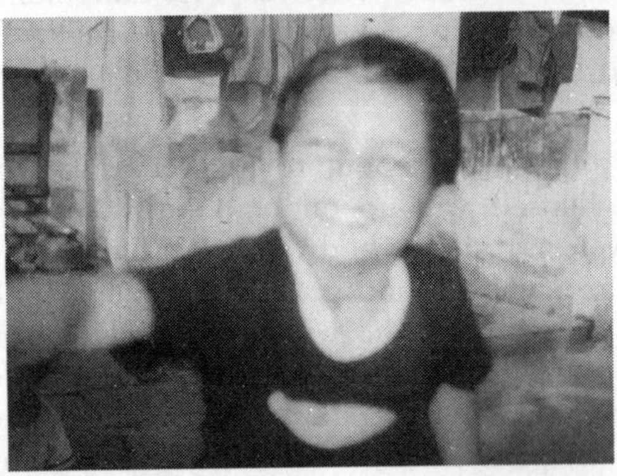

Remedial Measures

1. Develop psychomotor skills.
2. Give guidance to the child and to the parents.
3. Provide good speech therapy and behaviour modification therapy treatment by an expert.
4. Develop self-help skills by practice.
5. Arrange small group games frequently using ball.

CASE NO. 2: B. SAI SARAN

Sai Saran's father died. In the beginning Sai Saran's mother thought that he was a mentally retarded child and joined him in a mentally retarded school. Later they came to know from the teacher of the special school that he is not mentally retarded but autistic. The teacher realised this from his stereotyped behaviour. The boy likes to go to school everyday. As soon as he hears the school bus horn, he jumps out of the house and runs towards the bus. He sits in the bus very happily.

The investigator also observed him for a couple of days and carefully noted down all the activities and behaviour of the child. After making a clear study of the case, the boy was selected for indepth study.

Personal Data of the Child

Name	:	Batta Sai Saran
Class	:	Zero class
School	:	Chaitanya Manovikasa Kendram
Age	:	5th year
Sex	:	Male
Order of Birth	:	First
Caste	:	Padmasali
Religion	:	Hindu
Mother Tongue	:	Telugu
Place of Birth	:	Jandrapeta
Father's Name	:	B. Veerabhadra Rao (late)
Age	:	Died at the age of 43 years
Mother's Name	:	B. Leela Bramaramba
Age	:	33 years
Occupation	:	Weaver
Economic and Social Status	:	Poor
Type of House	:	Own Thatched house

Family Background

Sai Saran's father died when the child was four years of age. His mother shows mild autistic characters. His mother is illiterate and is afraid of talking to educated people. She is not even aware of the autistic disorder in her child. In her view her child is only mentally retarded. She lives in a thatched house and earns her living on weaving clothes. She joined her son in a mentally retarded school on the advice of a social worker. She is sincerely sending her child to school, with a whole-hearted hope to see her son as a normal child.

Genetic Factors

Sai Saran's parents are closely related. Sai Saran's delivery took place at home and it is a normal delivery. Sai Saran did not cry immediately after delivery. He took almost 15 minutes to cry. The doctors say that there is a chance of lack of oxygen supply to the brain, for which the child did not cry immediately. This may sometimes result in slight brain dysfunction.

His father died of cancer. Her mother also looks like a mild autistic person. Her response was very poor. Her language is also not clear. The words she spoke were difficult to comprehend. The researcher took the help of the school principal to collect the data.

Health Condition of the Case

Sai Saran is very lean and is dark in complexion. He has no eye contact. He will never look at us or talk to us. He always sits at the window and makes noises like stir, stir...etc. He will not recognise anybody other than his mother. He will neither speak nor utter meaningful words. He used to get fits at his childhood. He always moves his hands and whenever we stop him from moving his hands he will remain calm. But the moment we allow him to move his hands he does it more vigorously. He had good teeth. His nails are clean and neat. He looks like a 4 year old boy though he is 5 year old. Sai Saran will not concentrate on any work. He always likes to wave his hands by sitting at the window.

Communication Skills

Sai Saran cannot talk. But he has good memory power. He identifies the school van horn. He always likes to sit in the school van, go to school. Sai Saran cannot read and write. School teachers take a good care of him. He cannot respond to the teachers when they call out his name or he cannot tell his name. When the researcher tried to interview him he tried to swing her hands also in the same way.

Social Skills

Sai Saran never likes to meet anybody. He has no friends. He always likes to be with his mother in the school van or in the school. He doesn't like to come out of his world.

He didn't cry even when a person tries to intimidate him. He always likes to sit at the window swing his hands. The school headmistress expressed her opinion that the boy has high functional autistic characters. He does not show any emotions like fear, joy, anger, sadness, etc. He will never quarrel with others. He expects the school van even on Sunday.

Life skills

Sai Saran cannot eat anything on his own, either his mother, grandmother or the school aya must feed him the food. He cries when he is angry. Food must be juicy or in liquid form. He never eats solid food. If the food is not in liquid form, he pours a glass of water in it and then eats.

He doesn't know anything about toilet manners. He goes for motion wherever he likes. The school teachers are trying to teach him the toilet manners. He never harms or hurts anybody. He does not know what fear is. He is very cooperative at wearing clothes. He sleeps normally at night. He cries whenever he is hungry.

Brief Sketch of B. SAI SARAN (Case 2)

Causes	Symptoms
1) Sai Saran's parents are closely related.	1) No eye contact
2) Her mother also shows some autistic symptoms.	2) Appears to be deaf

3)	He was neglected, his father died and the family suffers from poverty.	3)	Do not play with peers
4)	There is delay in his physical and mental development.	4)	Do not respond to verbal sounds
		5)	Rocking his hands continuously one after another.
		6)	Do not show any interest in usual Activities
		7)	Have Elimination problem
		8)	Depends on others for daily routine work like personal cleanliness, eating, drinking, etc.

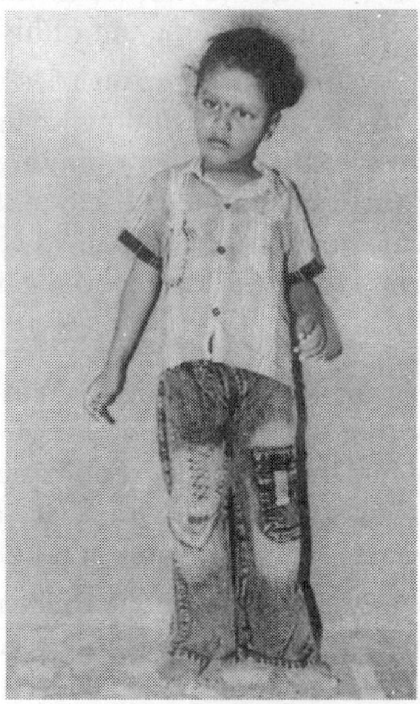

Remedial Measures

1. Develop psychomotor skills.
2. Pay special attention.
3. Give guidance to the parents and to the child.
4. Provide good speech therapy and behaviour modification therapy treatments by experts.
5. Develop self-help skills by practice.

6. Frequently arrange small group games to children by using ball, skipping rope, etc.

CASE NO. 3: S. SASIDHAR

Sasidhar is studying at Chaitanya Manovikasa Kendram at Chirala since one year. He didn't sit at one place. He always moves quickly from one place to other or climbs on the benches and disturb the items on the table. The parents thought that the child has got a mysterious disease. They tried various treatments and finally joined the child in the present school. The investigator observed him at school, at home and selected him for indepth study.

Personal Data of the Child

Name	:	Siddabathuni Sasidhar
Class	:	Zero class
School	:	Chaitanya Manovikasa Kendram
Age	:	6th year
Sex	:	Male
Order of Birth	:	First
Religion	:	Hindu
Mother Tongue	:	Telugu
Place of Birth	:	Guntur
Father's Name	:	Prakash
Age	:	30 years
Occupation	:	Working in an Advertising Agency
Mother's Name	:	Padmavathi, S.
Age	:	25 years
Occupation	:	Housewife
Economic and Social Status	:	Middle class
Type of House	:	Small rented house

Family Background

Sasidhar is the first born child to his parents. He lives in Chirala along with his maternal grandmother. Sasidhar's parents along with their second child live in Guntur. His father is a graduate and works in an advertising agency. His mother studied upto 10th class and is a housewife. As there is a free special education school available at Chirala, they kept him there. Everyday, Sasidhar goes to school from his grandmother's. They are living in a rented house in Chirala. They are a middle class family. Sasidhar is taken good care of by his grandmother.

Genetic Factors

At the time of pregnancy, Sasidhar's mother did not face any problems or risks. She gave birth normally but Sasidhar had not cried immediately after his birth. As a result the brain suffered the shortage of oxygen supply. This type of situation didn't happen to anyone in his family. As the time passes, the child has shown delayed physical and mental development. He didn't sit at one place for some time. He always tries to climb on a piece of furniture or a window.

Health Condition

The parents say that he is healthy but at the time of this investigation, he is suffering from jaundice. His eye ball is black. He has medium complexion. He has no fits.

Communication Skills

Sasidhar cannot speak. He cannot read and write. He cannot say his name. He has been attending to the special school for about a year. He likes the teacher. He is overactive, climbs on chairs, furniture, etc. He cannot speak words but produces some irregular and incoherent sounds. But he cannot understand the feelings of others but he can identify when the teacher or grandmother is angry. He communicates only through actions, signs, symbols for his necessities.

Social Skills

Sasidhar is a hyperactive child. He didn't stay stationary at one place. He didn't maintain any relationship with anybody except his grandmother and the school teacher. All the children of the special school settle down at one place whereas Sasidhar is seen struggling to climb a table (or) a chair. He never plays with other children. Clapping hands and uttering sounds like luu, luu,...etc., are his favourite activities. His eye contact is good.

Life Skills

Sasidhar was trained at school to take his food on his own. His food must consist of large or medium sized vegetable pieces otherwise he refuses to take food. Very carefully he picks up each piece with his two fingers and eats them. After all the pieces are over, he will eat rice with spoon. If anybody touches those pieces he immediately retaliates by beating with the spoon.

He was well trained in toilet manners at school. He uses the toilet very neatly and it took almost three months for the teachers to train him in this habit. He cannot brush his teeth or take a bath by himself. He always smiles.

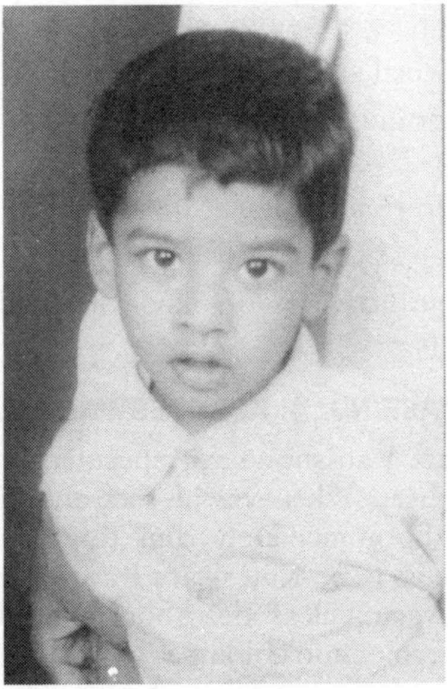

Brief Sketch of S. SASIDHAR (Case 3)

	Causes		Symptoms
1)	There is delayed physical and mental development	1)	Appears to be deaf

2)	His grandmother who is his present care taker is an uneducated woman and she thinks that this boy is mentally retarded	2)	Do not respond to verbal sounds
3)	He did not get balanced diet	3)	Do not play with peers
		4)	Hyperactive, moves constantly
		5)	Resort to spin and toe walking
		6)	Flop his hands
		7)	No interest in usual activities
		8)	Depends on others for daily routine activities
		9)	Sometimes he falls down and gets injured for no reason

Remedial Measures

1. Develop psychomotor skills.
2. Pay special attention to his needs.
3. Teacher must give constant guidance and support.
4. Provide good speech therapy and behaviour modification therapy.
5. Develop self-help skills by practice.
6. Arrange activities of play with ball, skipping rope, ring, etc.

CASE NO. 4: K. KOTESWARA RAO

K. Koteswara Rao shows very peculiar characteristics. He always helps others. Whenever he sees an elderly person with heavy luggage, he immediately runs towards them and helps them. The teachers of K. Koteswara Rao was in a dilemma and is not able to give any clear idea about him. He is very good at identifying vegetables and colours.

His parents are also of the confusion whether their child is mentally retarded or not. The boy shows interest in learning numbers and alphabets.

After careful observation by the investigator, and supported by doctors confirmation, the boy was taken for indepth study.

Personal Data of the Child

Name	:	Karapatti Koteswara Rao
Class	:	1st Class
School	:	Government Primary School, P.V.S. School, Perala
Age	:	10 years
Sex	:	Male
Order of Birth	:	First
Caste	:	Padmasali
Religion	:	Hindu
Mother Tongue	:	Telugu
Place of Birth	:	Chirala
Father's Name	:	Karapatti Subramanyam
Age	:	40 years
Occupation	:	Dying work – Daily labourer
Mother's Name	:	Karapatti Chowdeswari
Age	:	32 years
Occupation	:	Housewife
Economic and Social Status	:	Lower middle class
Type of House	:	Rented, tiled house

Family Background

The parents of Koteswara Rao are illiterates. They belong to lower middle class family. Koteswara Rao's mother always worries about her child because he is 10 years old, and he is still studying 1st standard. The family has good relationships with their neighbours and the neighbours also cooperate with the family member to develop the child. His father is a Kalankari (fabric paint) worker.

Genetic Factors

When Koteswara Rao's mother was pregnant she faced many problems. Her mother-in-law was not good towards her. She was very rude towards her and tortured her all the time. They belong to lower middle class family because of which many a time Koteswara Rao's mother went fasting even during pregnancy. She did not take any nutritive (or) balanced diet and this might have developed complications at delivery. The delivery was assisted with forceps. In later days doctors identified a tumour in his brain. His development was not proportionate to his age because of the brain tumour. He is still using medicines from neurospecialist.

Health Condition of the Case

Koteswara Rao is physically strong and has medium complexion. His eye ball is black and has black hair, but he is not always clean. He depends on the assistance of his mother for taking meals as well as bath. Most of the time, he plays in dust, and appears dusty. He gets fits occasionally. He has excellent memory. He could identify me even after three months though we met only once.

Communication Skills

Koteswara Rao can speak very fast. He often uses the word bye, bye. Though he is 10 years old, he is studying First Class at Government Primary School. He cannot differentiate one alphabet from the other. He is not interested in education. He talks to his neighbours. He loves to talk and play with puppies. He gathers all the puppies at his house and plays with them. He tries to interact with all the persons on the road with a smile.

Social Skills

Usually autistic children do not like to speak with others but Koteswara Rao makes friendship with all the people. He never stays at one place for 5 minutes. He always runs. In the classroom he didn't sit at one place and usually gets the ire of the teachers. He smiles at everyone. He plays with the children of all age groups. He loves to play with puppies. He is very helpful to others, only thing is, he cannot understand anything properly. He is a hyperactive child. He has very good relationship with his younger brother. His younger brother is like a guide to him. Both are close to their mother but they maintain some distance with their father. He is not afraid of strangers. He can't differentiate a boy from a girl. He sometimes calls a boy as girl and a girl as boy.

Life Skills

Koteswara Rao doesn't eat food by himself. His mother runs after him to make him eat the food. He didn't take food by sitting leisurely at one place. He is very selective in his food menu. He himself expressed his special interests when interviewed. He likes brinjal curry very much. In whatever way it is cooked, for example fry, curry or chutney he likes it. He has no eating manners and whenever his mother points out this, he simply says "bye", "bye" and refuses to take food.

He learned about toilet manners in his eighth year, with the assistance of his younger brother. Almost for 7 years, he could not tell about his toilet needs but slowly he is becoming normal. He sleeps normally.

He gets fits occasionally because of which the parents are very cautious about him. He seldom watches T.V., but when a program on puppies comes, he watches and tries to say something very fast, that is not understandable.

He is not interested in milk and junk foods. He didn't feel the sensation of hunger. His mother feeds him on time.

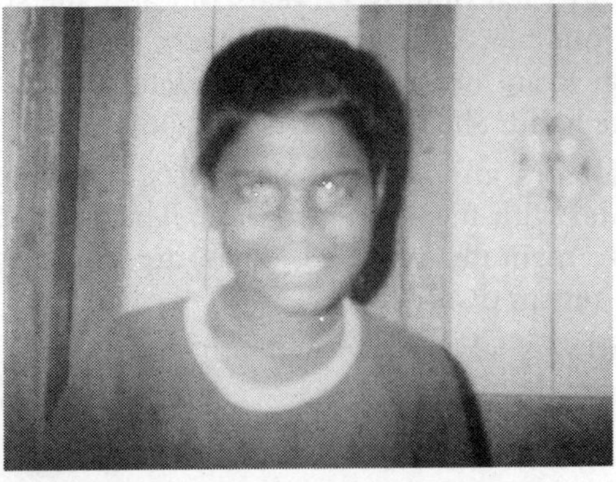

Brief Sketch of K. KOTESWARA RAO (Case 4)

	Causes		Symptoms
1)	His mother suffered nutrition deficiency as she didn't take good diet during pregnancy	1)	Moves continuously from place to place
2)	The delivery was done at home in unsafe conditions.	2)	Spin and run on his toes
3)	The child could not get sufficient diet	3)	Flop his hands
4)	The boy did not cry immediately after his birth	4)	No interest in usual activities
5)	He has a small tumour in his brain	5)	Depends on others for daily routine work like personal cleanliness eating, drinking, etc.
		6)	He constantly gets fits
		7)	He frequently gets injured

Remedial Measures

1. Develop psychomotor skills.
2. Pay special attention.
3. Educate the parents about the importance of nutrition and balanced diet for healthy living.
4. Provide behaviour modification therapy.
5. Develop self-help skills by practice.
6. Maintain good relationships with this boy.

CASE NO. 5: D. BHAGYA LAKSHMI

D. Bhagya Lakshmi is 12 years old and she stays at home. She sits at one place. She smiles at every one who meets her. If any person visits her regularly she identifies them and gives them shake hand. She never hurts anybody.

The doctors after neurological tests confirmed her as an autistic child with mental retardation. The parents believe that she is only mentally retarded. They are completely ignorant about her autism disorder.

The girl was taken up for indepth study.

Personal Data of the Child

Name	:	Damarla Bhagya Lakshmi
Class	:	Not yet joined in a school
Age	:	12 years
Sex	:	Female
Order of Birth	:	Second child
Caste	:	B.C.(B), Padmasali
Religion	:	Hindu
Mother Tongue	:	Telugu
Place of Birth	:	Perala
Father's Name	:	Damarla Venkateswara Prasad
Age	:	42 years
Occupation	:	Weaving
Mother's Name	:	Damarla Venkata Lakshmi
Age	:	28 years
Occupation	:	Housewife
Economic and Social Status	:	Middle class family
Type of House	:	Own, tiled roof house

Family Background

Bhagya Lakshmi's father studied upto 7th class. He works as a weaver. But he didn't show any interest in the upbringing of children. Bhagya Lakshmi is the second child to the parents. Their first child Tejeswari is normal and is studying in VIII Class. Bhagya Lakshmi's mother is an illiterate but she takes good care of her daughter. They did not have hereditary diseases. Both the parents are healthy and they are not closely related.

Genetic Factors

When Bhagya Lakshmi's mother was pregnant, her head was larger than normal size. Inspite of that, the delivery was normal. The child did not cry immediately after her birth. It resulted in short supply of oxygen to the brain. She has delayed physical and mental development. The family has no history of this type of child birth earlier.

Health Condition of the Case

Bhagya Lakshmi is 12 years old and she is healthy, clean and neat. Her nails are clean. But she doesn't have any knowledge of her feminine nature. Hence, her mother dresses her like a boy and cut her hair to look like a boy. As the child is nearing adolescence her mother took this precaution as she does not know how to cover body decently. Her physical growth is proportionate to her age with black eye ball and dark skin.

Communication Skills

Bhagya Lakshmi cannot speak. She cannot cry even. She remains silent to express her anger She always greets the other people with a smile. Her mother makes her sit on the veranda everyday. She looks at the passers by with a smile. If anybody smiles in return, she identifies them and shows a change in the smile. But she stays wherever her mother puts her. She didn't drift to any side. She doesn't know the difference between boy and girl. She is not afraid of animals or birds. The communication skills she uses are clapping hands and girding smile. She uses different smile types for different expressions.

Social Skills

Bhagya Lakshmi tries to interact with others. Her mother makes her sit in the veranda so that she can see all the people. In the earlier days, Bhagya Lakshmi's parents used to tither her in the house thinking that their child is mentally retarded. After the doctors confirmed that she is autistic and not mentally retarded, they stopped tithering her. The child can identify the persons she met. She tries to play with other children. Whenever a person meets her she claps her hands and make the other person clap by grabbing their hands.

Life Skills

Though Bhagya Lakshmi is 12 years old, she cannot eat on her own. Her mother helps her in eating food. She has no special interest in her food. She does not show any interest even to take food on time. She just smiles whatever that tastes salty, sweet, bitter or spicy. But from the type of smile her mother can understand whether she likes the food or not.

Bhagya Lakshmi was given toilet training by her mother. Her mother remembers the timings and instructs her to use the toilet. In case, if she ever forgets to instruct her, she urinates wherever she is. Bhagya Lakshmi was not sent to any school. She is not given any therapies or interventions. They are using only medicines. In her parents view, she is just a mentally retarded child. The researcher educated her mother about Bhagya Lakshmi's state, the treatments, the therapies and the interventions that are available to make her a normal child. Her mother gained a lot of confidence after the researcher's guidance and advice.

Brief Sketch of D. BHAGYA LAKSHMI (Case 5)

	Causes		Symptoms
1)	She did not cry immediately after her birth	1)	Appears to be deaf
2)	She has a little bit of brain problem	2)	Flop hands
3)	Delayed mental development	3)	No interest in usual activities
4)	Her mother did not take good care during pregnancy	4)	Depend on others for daily routine work like personal cleanliness, eating, drinking, etc.
		5)	She gets fits

Remedial Measures

1. Develop psychomotor skills.
2. Pay special attention to the child.
3. Provide good speech therapy and behaviour modification therapy.
4. Develop self-help skills.
5. Give special education and training for future life.

CASE NO. 6: A. SAMUYELU

Samuyelu is 16 years old and a drop out from school due to his mischievous behaviour. He has no friends. His age mates told the researcher that he is an energetic boy. He is good at drawing and identifying the origin of sounds. He produces unique sounds which they had never heard before from anyone. His parents are of the opinion that he is not mentally retarded. He helps his parents in running their cycle repair shop. He can attend to his personal things by himself. His sisters also love him very much. He has improper speech and cannot utter words properly.

After careful observation by the researcher, the boy was taken up for indepth study.

Personal Data of the Child

Name	:	Allamudi Samuyelu
Education	:	Drop out from school without any education
Age	:	16 years
Sex	:	Male
Order of Birth	:	First
Caste	:	S.C.
Religion	:	Hindu
Mother Tongue	:	Telugu

Place of Birth	:	Repalle
Father's Name	:	Allamudi Prabhudasu
Age	:	48 years
Occupation	:	Cycle repair shop
Mother's Name	:	Allamudi Mariyamma
Age	:	32 years
Occupation	:	Housewife
Economic and social status	:	Lower middle class
Type of House	:	Own thatched house

Family Background

Samuyelu's father is an uneducated person and his mother studied upto Vth Class. They live in their own thatched house and belong to lower middle class. Samuyelu's father works in a small cycle shop. Samuyelu is 16 years old. They never sent him to any school. He too works in the cycle shop. He is good at the repair work. Samuyelu has got two younger sisters and they are normal. Samuyelu's family members have good relationships with their neighbours.

Genetic Factors

Samuyelu's mother did not face any problem at the time of pregnancy or delivery. But the family has a history of children of this type being born to their ancestors. His mental development is less than his age and physical development. All the family members are healthy and strong and have no other health problems.

Health Condition of the Case

Samuyelu is physically strong and healthy. He is 4 feet 5 inches tall and the colour of his eye ball is black. His has grey hair. He never combs his hair. He looks like a 16 year boy but he behaves like a 6 year old child. He used to get fits when he was a small child. His parents are not using any medicines, they believe in spiritual healing. He has good eye contact. He is not clean. He appears dusty and he never wears clean clothes.

Communication Skills

Samuyelu speaks very less with others. He cannot spell the words properly. He tries to speak but his voice is not clear. He tries to speak to his younger sisters. He didn't go to school that's why he cannot read and write. He has not shown any interest in writing or drawing. The researcher asked him to draw an object which she has drawn but he refused to draw it. When the researcher has drawn some circles he drew them. Slowly beginning with small and simple objects, he has shown interest in drawing objects and figures like apple, snake, fish, etc. While drawing fish the researcher has drawn the fish without fins but Samuyelu corrected it and drew the fish with fins and scales and smiled at the researcher.

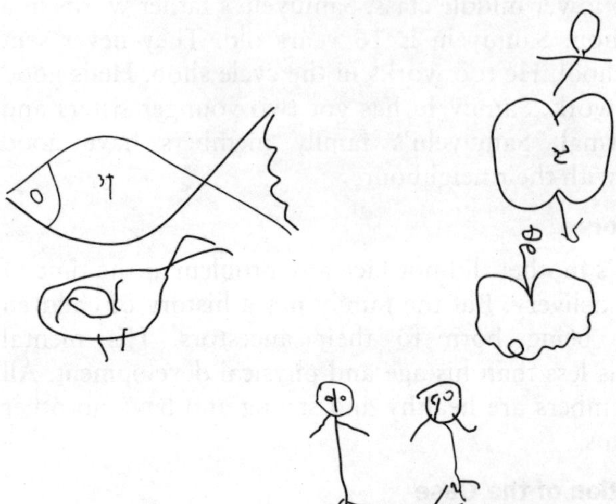

Samuyelu has drawn these pictures with greater speed than the researcher. This indicates his interest in drawing and the accuracy of his observation.

Social Skills

Samuyelu moves closely with his parents, sisters and his only friend. He never tries to talk to strangers. It is tough time for the researcher to make him respond to her. She could make him talk through his favourite drawing skills. He is very much interested in observing nature and surroundings. At the cycle shop, he works very sincerely. He is a hyperactive boy. In his childhood when his parents joined him in a school he has thrown a stone at a boy. The boy lost his eyesight. The parents are afraid of his activities and dropped him from the school. When the researcher asked him about this incidence he laughed aloud and said friend, friend....

Life Skills

He can do his work on his own. Brushing teeth and taking bath are guided by his sisters. He don't know about gender distinction. He likes non-vegetation food. He goes on circling the kitchen when his mother cooks fish. He is stubborn and likes to eat large quantities. He likes junk food.

It took eight long years to teach him the toilet manners. Though he is 16 years old his life skills are poor and his father often beats him for his abnormal behaviour.

Brief Sketch of Case 6

Causes	Symptoms
1. The family has the history of the birth of this type of children	1. Lack of clarity in speech and words. Suffering from echolalia
2. Delay in mental development	2. Do not like to mix with age peers
3. Father is careless and did not know the importance of nutritious food	3. Do not sit at one place for some time
4. Normal house delivery with the supervision of an untrained maid	4. Hyperactive boy
	5. Do not show much interest in usual activities
	6. He gets fits occasionally
	7. Depend on others for daily routine work like personal cleanliness, eating, drinking, etc.

Remedial Measures

1. Pay special attention.

2. Educate him and give guidance to him.
3. Develop and give training in social skills.
4. Provide speech therapy.
5. Develop self-help skills by practice.

SUGGESTIONS TO THE PARENTS

1. Parents are suggested to provide the basic needs of the children.
2. Parents are advised to live with their children, spend some time with them and share the joys and sorrows of their children.
3. Parents should train their children and give their full co-operation to develop self-help skills.
4. Parents must provide good parent-child relationship and good home environment.
5. Parents must strictly avoid comparing their children with other normal children.
6. Parents must bring up their children themselves and should not pass on their responsibility to others.
7. Parents are suggested to avoid criticism and resort to praise or reward on successful completion of even a small task.
8. Parents should think of helping and supporting their children in a number of ways.
9. They are suggested to have patience in bringing up their children.

SUGGESTIONS TO THE TEACHERS

1. Teachers are suggested to take individual care and discuss with the parents about child's progress in the development of skills and studies.
2. They are suggested to plan activities in which all the students of autism can participate.
3. The school medical officer, psychiatrist, behaviour therapist and speech therapist should provide expert guidance.

4. Teachers must develop self-help skills.
5. Patience is necessary on the part of teachers. They are suggested to take good care and nurse the autistic children.

OUTCOMES OF THE STUDY

1. The case studies of autistic children provide information on the characteristics, nature, and behaviours of ASD children.
2. Specific and general outcomes of children with autistic features are available.
3. Specific and general remedial measures for those children suffering from autism are available.
4. Six case studies of mild, moderate, high functional autism with mental retardation are available.
5. This information helps in planning remedial measures and enriching the existing programmes.
6. Problems and needs of autistic children in general are made available.
7. It helps in proposing different theories for the onset of autism.
8. It helps in devising treatments, methods and gadgets to mitigate the problems of autism children.

SUGGESTIONS FOR FURTHER RESEARCH

1. Follow up studies on different cases of autistic children can be taken up.
2. Case studies of children with serious autistic, psychological and sociological problems can be taken up.
3. A case study of both trainable and educable autistic children can be compared and general remedial measures can be suggested for the teachers and the parents.
4. The study of behavioural problems of autistic children can be taken up.

5. There are many causes of autism. Students can be taken up on the causes of autism.

CONCLUSION

Out of the present study, the following conclusions are drawn. R. Bhanu Ganesh and K. Koteswara Rao are having mild features of autism. Sasidhar and Samuyelu have moderate features of autism. Sai Saran is a high functional autistic boy and Bhagya Lakshmi is an autistic girl with metal retardation.

Bhanu Ganesh and Samuyelu have high rate of I.Q. Sai Saran has no eye contact. Except Koteswara Rao, all the children are suffering from speech problems. All the children are suffering from behavioural problems. Bhanu Ganesh, Sasidhar, Koteswara Rao and Samuyelu are hyperactive children, Sai Saran and Bhagya Lakshmi simply sits at one place. All need speech therapy and behaviour therapy. The autistic children are entirely different from mentally retarded children. They show different characteristics.

Bibliography

Books

Anderson, A.S., et al. (1987). *Intensive Home-based Early Intervention with Autistic Children*, Education and Treatment of Children, 10.

Andrew, Nelson (2008). *Social Skills for Individuals with Asperger Syndrome*. 1st Edition, Prachee Publications, Hyderabad.

Barlinge, M.K. (1977). *A Study of Influence of Mother's Personality of Child's Personality*, in Buch M.B., (Ed.), Second Survey of Research in Education, Baroda.

Bondy, A. and Frost, L. (2002). *A Picture's Worth: PECS and Other Visual Communications Strategies in Autism*. MD: Woodbine House, Bethesda.

Dawson, G. and Osterling, J. (1997). "Early Intervention in Autism" in M. Guralnick (Ed.). *The Effective of Early Intervention*. M.D: Paul H. Brooker, Baltimore.

Marian, Sigman and Lisa, Capps (1997). *Children with Autism: A Developmental Perspective*. Cambridge Harvard University Press, Cambridge.

Mythily, Charia and Salyam, Chari (2008). *Educational Management of Students with Autism Spectrum Disorders*. 1st Edition, Prachee Publications, Hyderabad.

Prithvi, Perepa (2007). *Autism*. Ist Edition. Prachee Publications, Hyderabad.

Quill, K.A. (2000). *Do-Waten-Listen-Say: Social and Communication Intervention for Children with Autism*. Baltimore, Paul H. Brooker, Baltimore.

Richard, L. Simpson (2008). *Autism Spectrum Disorders*, Sage Publications India Private Limited (Sage South Asia Edition), New Delhi.

Savner, J.L. and Myles, B.S. (2000). *Making Visual Supports Work in the Home and Community: Strategies for Individuals with Autism and Asperger Syndrom*. Shawnee Mission, KS: Autism Asperger.

Journals

Bernard, Optiz V., Siriam, N. and Nakhoda-Sapuan, S. (2001). "Enhancing social problem solving in children with autism and normal children through computer- assisted instruction." *Journal of Autism and Developmental Disorders*, 31(4), pp. 377-84.

Elliott, R.O., Hall, K. and Soper, H.V. (1991). "Analog language teaching versus, natural language teaching: Generalisation and retention of language learning for adults with autism and mental retardation." *Journal of Autism and Developmental Disorders*. 21(4), pp. 433-46.

Green, G. (1996). "Early behavioural intervention for autism—What does research tell us?" in C. Maurica G. Green and S.C. Luce (Eds.). *Behavioural Intervention for Young Children with Autism—A Manual for Parents and Professionals, Austin*, TXL: PRO-Ed, pp. 29-44.

Jones, R.S.P. and M.C. Caughey, R.E. (1992). "Gentle Teaching and Applied Behaviour Analysis: A Critical Review." *Journal of Applied Behavioural Analysis*, 25(40), pp. 853-67.

McGee, G.G., Daly, T. and Jacobs, H.A. (1984). "The Walden Preschool" in S.L. Harris and J.S. Handleman (Eds.) *Preschool Education Programs for Children with Autism*, Autism TX: pro-Ed., pp. 127-62.

Ritvo, E.R. and Freeman, B.J. (1978). "National Society for Autistic Children, Definition of the Syndrome of Autism", *Journal of Autism and Childhood, Schizophrenia*, 8, pp. 162-69.

Shiort, A.B. (1984). "Short-term treatment outcome using parents as co-therapists for their own autistic children", *Journal of Child Psychiatry and Allied Disciplines*, 25(3), pp. 443-58.

Sugai, G. and White, W. (1986). "The Effects of Using Object Stimulation as a Reinforcer on the Prevocational Work Rates of an Autistic Child" in *The Journal of Autism and Other Developmental Disabilities*, 16(4), pp. 459-71.

Thorp, D.M., Stahmer, A.C. and Schereibman, L. (1995). "Effects of Socio-dramatic Play Training on Children with Autism" in *Journal of Autism and Developmental Disorders*, 25(3), pp. 265-82.

Internet Sources

Abbie Solish (2007), "Participation of Children with and without Disabilities in Social Recreational and Leisure Activities," 08/04/2010, http//asdcarc.com/index.php/publisher/articiereview/frmArticielD/333

Ananda Laxmy, S. (1982), "Cognitive Competence in Infancy," 8/4/2010, http://www.education.nic.in/cd50 years/g/z/9I/ 0Z910902.htm

Desai, K.G. (1985), "Learning Disabilities of Primary School Children," Department of Education, Ministry of Human Resource Development, Government of India, 8/4/2010, http://www.education.nic.in/cd50years/g/z/9i/0z9i0705.htm

Kalra, N. (1979), Patterns of psychological problems of children 5-13 years—their etiology and symptomatology, http://www.education.nic.in/cd50years/g/z/9j/0Z9J0E01.htm

Kristen Mc Fee (2009), "Understanding the Symbolic Nature of Pictures in Children with Autism," 8/2/2010, http//asdcarc.com/index.php/publisher/articlereview/frm ArticleID/344

Lalitha Ramanujan (2010), "Social Adaptability and Social Skill Training," 8/4/2010, Institute for Remedial Intervention Services, www.autismindia.com/articlel.htm

Lindsay Arnal (2009), "Can Tutors Learn to Teach Children with Autism Through Self-instruction?," 8-4-2010, http//asdcarc.com/index.php/publisher/articlereview/frm ArticlelD/345

Mallya, I.P. (1982), "Special Play Session—A Playway Method to help Children with Special Needs." Dept. of Child Development, MSU, Baroda, (ICSSR financed), 3/1/2010, http://www.education.nic.in/cd50vears/g/z/9i/0Z9J0E02.htm

Mazumdar, N.A. (2010), "Management of Autism: A Parent's Perspective," 8/4/2010, Institute for Remedial Intervention Services (I.R.I.S.), www.autismindia.com/ articlel6.htm

Michael Waldman (2008), "Evidence of Major Environmental Trigger for Autism," 8/4/2010, PHYSorg.com, http://www.physorg.com/news 145544025.html

Index